disc

Looking Closely

across the Desert

FRANK SERAFINI

Kids Can Press

Look very closely.

What do you see?

A pincushion?
Monster skin?
What could it be?

It's a Prickly Pear Cactus.

A prickly pear cactus can grow as high as 3.5 m (12 ft.) tall. It sprouts green cactus pads shaped like beaver tails. Yellow, red or purple flowers bloom along the edges of the pads.

In the late spring, the cactus's flowers drop off, making room for spiky purple fruit to swell and burst, releasing their seeds. People use these prickly pears to make jam, jelly and candy.

Look very closely.

What do you see?

An eagle's foot?
A witch's claw?
What could it be?

It's a *Spiny Lizard.*

Spiny lizards blend perfectly into their desert surroundings. They hide in cracks and burrows to avoid being eaten by hawks, owls and snakes. They use their sharp claws to climb rocks and trees while hunting for insects.

Their color also helps them survive the desert weather. When it gets cold, the lizard's scales grow dark to absorb the sun's heat. In summer, its scales lighten to reflect sunlight and keep the lizard cool.

Look very closely.

What do you see?

Cornsilk?
A lion's mane?
What could it be?

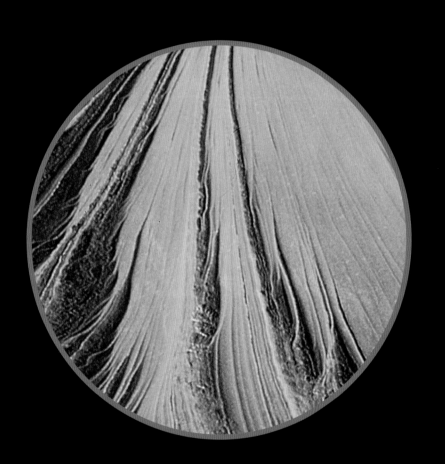

It's a *Sandstone* Wave.

Sandstone is made from ancient sand dunes, riverbeds and ocean floors. In these places, over millions of years, layer after layer of sand built up. As the sand piled on, the bottom layers were pressed together until they turned into rock.

Some sandstone is soft, allowing the wind, rain and ice to carve shapes into its face. Other sandstone is hard enough to use as building stones. If you look closely at a piece of sandstone, you can see grains of sand from long ago.

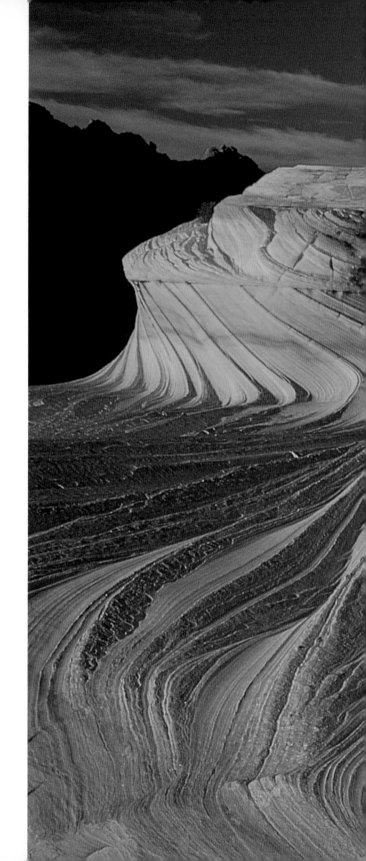

Look very closely.

What do you see?

A birthday candle?
A toothpick?
What could it be?

It's a Saguaro Cactus Flower.

The towering saguaro cactus stands guard over the desert. It can grow taller than a house and weigh over two tons. But the cactus grows slowly. It takes fifty years for a saguaro cactus to sprout flowers for the first time.

When in bloom, the saguaro looks as if it is wearing a white flower bonnet. Each flower blooms once, opening at night and closing the next morning. During the night, long-nosed bats dip their tongues into the flower's sweet nectar. Like bees, the bats carry pollen to all the other flowers they visit.

Look very closely.

What do you see?

A sand dune?
A snowy hill?
What could it be?

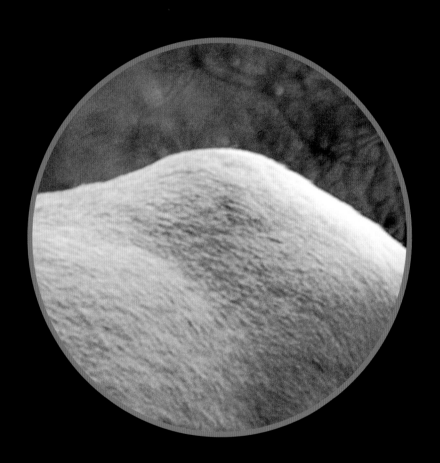

It's a Desert Bighorn Sheep.

Desert bighorn sheep get their name from the massive, curly horns on their heads. It takes seven to eight years for male bighorn sheep, or rams, to grow a full set of horns. Males butt heads to see who is the leader of the herd. Female bighorn sheep, or ewes, have smaller, shorter horns.

With their rubbery hoof pads, desert bighorn sheep can walk along sheer cliffs and leap from ledge to ledge. They can go for several days without water, which helps them live through the dry desert summers.

Look very closely.

What do you see?

A yellow spider?
A golden crown?
What could it be?

It's a Gold Poppy.

Gold poppies bring vibrant colors to the desert. If it rains a lot in the winter, gold poppies carpet the desert ravines come spring. If it doesn't rain much, only a few poppies will dot the landscape.

Gold poppies have no fragrance, but attract bees and insects with their bright colors. These short-stemmed flowers only need a little water to live. They can survive where other flowers cannot.

Look very closely.

What do you see?

Dinosaur teeth?
A zipper?
What could it be?

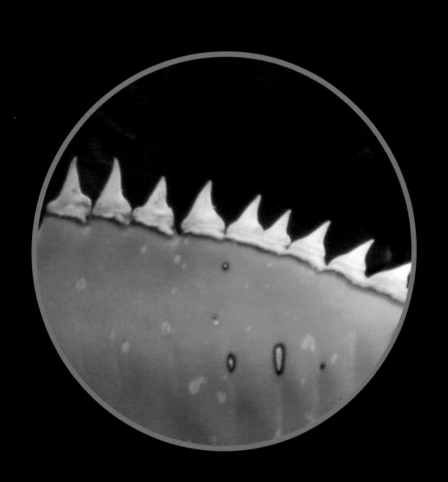

It's an Agave.

Agaves grow in spirals close to the ground. Their leaves have sharp edges and pointy ends that keep away nosy people and hungry animals. Agaves are related to cactus. Like cactus, agaves have a waxy coating to hold in water during the dry summer months.

Desert dwellers use agaves in many ways. Some kinds of agaves are used for weaving baskets. Others are used for medicine and cooking.

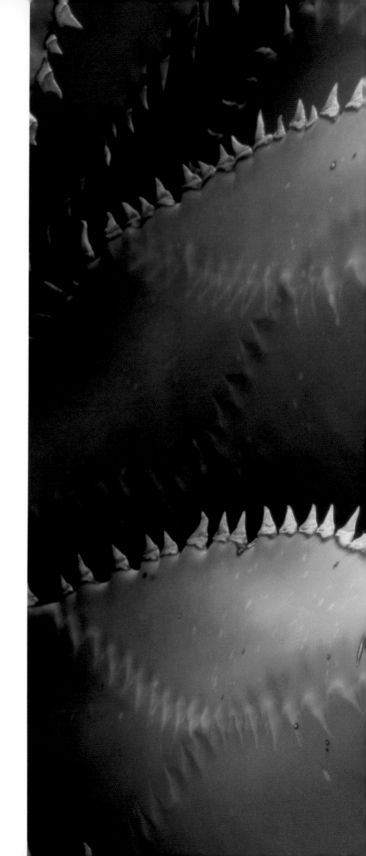

Look very closely.

What do you see?

A suit of armor?
A fossil or feathers?
What could it be?

It's a Diamondback Rattlesnake.

The diamondback rattlesnake gets its name from the diamond-shaped marks along its back. Diamondbacks are the largest rattlesnake and can grow to 2 m (7 ft.) long. These snakes can live over twenty-five years.

Rattlesnakes warn their enemies to stay away by shaking the rattle on the end of their tails. These snakes use poison, or venom, in their fangs to paralyze their prey before swallowing it whole.

Look very closely.

What do you see?

A glacier?
An ocean?
What could it be?

It's a White Sand Dune.

One quarter of all desert areas are covered in sand. Sand is made of broken down pieces of rocks, minerals and even seashells. Sand is blown across the desert by the wind and piles up in dunes.

When wind blows across sand dunes, it creates ripples in the sand like water. Once the wind changes direction, the sand is wiped clean for new patterns to appear.

Dedicated to my desert friends, Lyn, Buz, Todd and Kay

Photographer's Note

Photographers pay attention to things that most people overlook or take for granted. I can spend hours wandering along the shore, through the forest, across the desert or in my garden, looking for interesting things to photograph. My destination is not a place, but rather a new way of seeing.

It takes time to notice things. To be a photographer, you have to slow down and imagine in your "mind's eye" what the camera can capture. Ansel Adams said you could discover a whole life's worth of images in a six-square-foot patch of Earth. In order to do so, you have to look very closely.

By creating the images featured in this series of picture books, I hope to help people attend to nature, to things they might have normally passed by. I want people to pay attention to the world around them, to appreciate what nature has to offer, and to begin to protect the fragile environment in which we live.

Text and photographs © 2008 Frank Serafini

Pages 38–39: Mazatzal Mountains, USA   Back cover: Mojave National Preserve, USA

Kids Can Press acknowledges the financial support of the Government of Ontario, through the Ontario Media Development Corporation's Ontario Book Initiative.

Published in Canada by
Kids Can Press Ltd.
29 Birch Avenue
Toronto, ON M4V 1E2

Published in the U.S. by
Kids Can Press Ltd.
2250 Military Road
Tonawanda, NY 14150

www.kidscanpress.com

Edited by Karen Li
Designed by Julia Naimska
Printed and bound in China

This book is smyth sewn casebound.

CM 08 0 9 8 7 6 5 4 3 2 1

Library and Archives Canada Cataloguing in Publication

Serafini, Frank
Looking closely across the desert / Frank Serafini.

(Looking closely)
ISBN 978-1-55453-211-7

1. Desert biology—Juvenile literature. I. Title. II. Title: Across the desert. III. Series: Looking closely (Toronto, Ont.)

QH88.S47 2008   578.754   C2007-905567-2

Kids Can Press is a *corus* ™ Entertainment company